Joseph and His Brothers

Pictures by Kelly Pulley

Jacob had many sons.

Dear Parent:
Your child's love of reading starts here!

Every child learns to read in a different way and at his or her own speed. Some go back and forth between reading levels and read favorite books again and again. Others read through each level in order. You can help your young reader improve and become more confident by encouraging his or her own interests and abilities. From books your child reads with you to the first books he or she reads alone, there are I Can Read Books for every stage of reading:

SHARED READING
Basic language, word repetition, and whimsical illustrations, ideal for sharing with your emergent reader

BEGINNING READING
Short sentences, familiar words, and simple concepts for children eager to read on their own

READING WITH HELP
Engaging stories, longer sentences, and language play for developing readers

READING ALONE
Complex plots, challenging vocabulary, and high-interest topics for the independent reader

I Can Read Books have introduced children to the joy of reading since 1957. Featuring award-winning authors and illustrators and a fabulous cast of beloved characters, I Can Read Books set the standard for beginning readers.

A lifetime of discovery begins with the magical words "I Can Read!"

*Visit www.icanread.com for information
on enriching your child's reading experience.*

**Visit www.zonderkidz.com/icanread for more faith-based
I Can Read! titles from Zonderkidz.**

Joseph's brothers saw that their father
loved him more than any of them.
So they hated Joseph. They couldn't even
speak one kind word to him.
—*Genesis 37:4*

ZONDERKIDZ

Joseph and His Brothers
Copyright © 2008 by Zondervans. All Rights Reserved. All Beginner's Bible copyrights
and trademarks (including art, text, characters, etc.) are owned by Zondervan of
Grand Rapids, Michigan.

Requests for information should be addressed to:
Zonderkidz, 3900 Sparks Drive SE, Grand Rapids, Michigan 49546

ISBN 978-0-310-71731-7

All Scripture quotations unless otherwise noted are taken from The Holy Bible,
New International Reader's Version®, NIrV®. Copyright © 1995, 1996, 1998 by Biblica,
Inc.® Used by permission. All rights reserved worldwide.

Any internet addresses (websites, blogs, etc.) and telephone numbers printed in
this book are offered as a resource. They are not intended in any way to be or imply
an endorsement by Zondervan, nor does Zondervan vouch for the content of these
sites and numbers for the life of this book.

Zonderkidz is a trademark of Zondervan.

I Can Read® and I Can Read Book® are trademarks of HarperCollins Publishers.

Art Direction & Design: Jody Langley

He loved Joseph the best.

Jacob gave Joseph a robe.

Joseph's brothers were mad.

They wanted a robe too.

One day, Joseph took food
to his brothers in the fields.

"Last night, I had a dream,"
said Joseph.

"You all bowed down to me."

Some of his brothers
didn't like Joseph's dream.
They wanted to hurt Joseph.

One brother said,
"Do not hurt him.
Let's send him away."

They sold Joseph to some men.

The men took Joseph far away.

Joseph was put in jail.

But God took care of Joseph.

Joseph met a man in jail.

The man said,

"I used to work for the king."

The man said,

"Last night, I had a dream.

I gave a drink to the king."

"What does my dream mean?"
the man asked.

"God knows about your dream. It means you will work for the king again," said Joseph.

Joseph was right.

A few days later,

the man got out of jail.

The man went to work
for the king again.

Soon the king had a dream.
"What does it mean?" he said.

"Joseph can tell you what
your dream means,"
said the man.

The king let Joseph
out of jail.

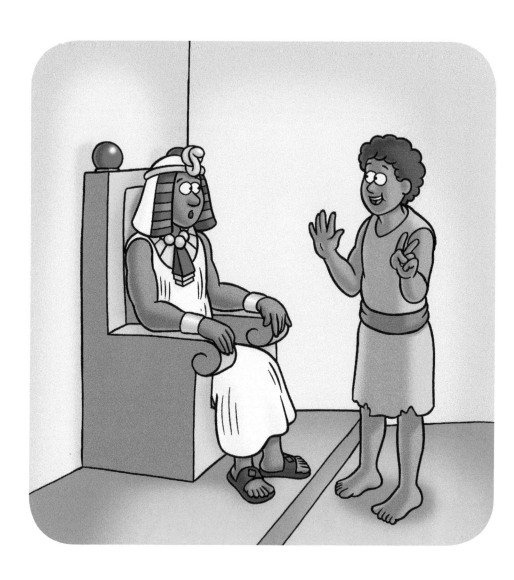

Joseph said, "Lots of food
will grow for seven years.
Then food will stop growing.

God wants us to save food now
so we won't be hungry later."
So the people saved up food.

Joseph was right.
After seven years, the food
stopped growing.

Joseph's family had no food.

They went to the king for help.

The brothers bowed to Joseph.
They did not know it was him.

"I am your brother!"
Joseph said.

"Do not be scared.
I forgive you," said Joseph.
"This was part of God's plan.

God sent me here to help.
God's people did not go hungry,"
said Joseph.

"God is good!"
Joseph and his brothers
cheered.